High Season
Poems and Musings

High Season

Poems and Musings

Carol Ann Nasta

New York

Copyright © 2022 Carol Ann Nasta

ISBN 978-1-956474-04-6 paperback
ISBN 978-1-956474-03-9 eBook

All rights reserved. No part of this book may be reproduced or transmitted in any form or by any means, electronic or mechanical, including photocopying, recording or by an information storage or retrieval system now known or hereafter invented—except by a reviewer who may quote brief passages in a review to be printed in a magazine or newspaper—without permission in writing from the publisher: heliotropebooks@gmail.com

Cover Painting by Carol Ann Nasta
Type Design by Carol Ann Nasta and Jonny Warschauer

To Helene, my cat Festus, and our planet
with its stunning array of wildlife
and natural beauty.

CONTENTS

FAMILY	13
The Photo	15
Young Jeanine and Me	16
Villanelle for Louis	18
Family Secret	19
Comfort	20
The Doorway	21
Mother's Way	22
Missing 1	27
Missing 2	27
A Child's Dream	28
"Very early in life it was too late"	29
My Inheritance	31
SEASONS; SEASONS WITHIN	33
Autumn	35
In Autumn	35
In Autumn 2	36
A Walk in Central Park: Autumn	37
Winter	38
Christmas Clear	38
From the Metro North Hudson Line in Winter	39
Black Ice	40
Spring	42
Life Force	42
Summer	43
I Am Summer	43
Call	44
Tranquility	45
Essence	46
The Gift	47

Summer Laze	49
A Time	50
From My Inside Jungle in Summer	52
Never Too Much	54
SHORTER POEMS and MUSINGS	57
Varied	57
Dated Angst Years	66
Haikus	71
MIXED THEMES	73
Homescapes: Apartment, Street, City	75
Elephant Ear	75
Mourning Cloak Butterfly	76
Sunset/Dusk from My Roof	78
My Street's Linden Tree	79
The City	80
City Lines	81
City Lines Revised	81
Human-made	82
"Far from the madding crowd"	83
My Street in Progress 1	84
My Street in Progress 2	88
Street Feast	90
My Habitat	91
Friends	92
Sestina for My Friend	93
Silence	94
A Visit (Revised from *End*)	96
Elegy for Rosie	98
Aliens	99
Lovers	102
Fantasy on "Romeo and Juliet"	102
Refuge	103
Favorite Lover	104
Heat	106
Him	107
Remembered	111

9/11	112
Thoughts on September 11	112
After Effects	113
Commemoration Day	114
Saturday September 14th. Epilogue	115
All Mixed	116
Writings From Line quotes From	
Ash Wednesday by T. S. Eliot	116
Stream of Conscious, Stream of Color	118
At Sixteen	119
Mirrors	120
On the Beach	122
Palisades	123
My Blouse	124
Mysteries	125
Butterfly Conservatory	126
Country Road	127
Reverie	128
THOUGHTS ON HUMAN NATURE	131
Litany and Rhyme to Human Nature	133
Dead End	136
A Jaundiced-eye View in "Couplets"	
of Contradiction	137
Anthropocene	140
PROSE PIECES	142
For People Who are Afraid of Others	145
Dressing with Feeling	146
Observations on Psychological Phenomena..Time	147
The Flame	148
Wednesday, 9/11 Commemoration A Year Later	149
The Girls	152
Momentum	154
FAVORITE QUOTES	156
FAVORITE SONG LYRICS	158

FAMILY

THE PHOTO

Her eyes smile
Even when she doesn't.
There are eyes like that.
It's visceral—
Is it shape, color, lashes,
Vertical width of the lids?

No, the whole is greater.

Or is she shining through?
That unanalyzable self
    Irreducible
But—the physical is so *there*.
    For the rest of us to
    attribute to
    associate with
    fantasize about
    Misinterpret.

I don't know.
    Can't explain.
It's just her eyes.
    They're like that.

YOUNG JEANINE AND ME

She and I live
    in the moment of a laugh,
Loves my company
Likes to wear my clothes.
Revives my childhood—
Play, laughter, fun
    Shaken, grayed
By my sister's chronic
    illness.
            Me
Fraught with worry—
    an amorphous threat lurked.
Fragility could shatter us.
Panic—someone will die.
    Who knows when.

This lovely child provides
Play, laughter fun lost
On a distant time line.

She told me
    I feel like her sister—
        almost half a century
    between—
The between means little.

She is my cousin
    twice removed.
The removal means nothing.
Blood is thick.
    Spirit can be thicker.

She reminds me of me
                as a child.
Playful, often inward-turned.
Slim, imaginative, dreamy, sensitive.
She pouts and cries at school
    Over unspoken hurts and fears.
I brooded, shook, couldn't sleep
    Over unspoken hurts and fears.

VILLANELLE FOR LOUIS

Slowly he had walked away
With the little one on the chilled lawn.
His massive form usually holds sway.

As he guarded the little one at play,
From a distance we looked on.
Slowly he had walked away.

My perception changed that day.
He seemed to be forlorn.
His massive form usually holds sway.

As if a colossal structure of clay
From a distance aura lessened, bulk gone.
Slowly he'd walked away.

Isolated, wistful from far away.
Often intimidating to gaze upon.
His massive form usually holds sway.

I was wrapped in dismay.
Was true vision in its dawn?
Slowly he had walked away.
His massive form usually held sway.

FAMILY SECRET

Outsized beds   A dark bedroom
Big bulging bureau
I entered, moved clumsily
Close to clunky objects
    Stifling space
I opened a closet
Cramped garment-beings pressed outward
Consumed every wisp of air
    I hyperventilated,
        and

Escaped
    To the living room   No escape
No empty spaces
Sagging sofa
Imposing piano
Ample armchairs
Large lampshades
                Small room.

COMFORT

I am supposed to let go—
    let go of corpses.
Closure gets easily locked in a vacant room.

Lazarus turns handsome, robust
    his impurities cleansed in
the fluid of Mind's desire.

My arms enfold him—once again.
    Nothing dies.
My house is crowded with ghosts.

I'm bolstered by diaphanous warmth.

THE DOORWAY

I stood in the doorway
    half-naked, half in darkness.
I didn't know what to expect.
Everything in shadow—
Was the bed occupied?
Was a ghost there? A body
    under the covers?

      Was it you?

I was a stranger, leaning
Against the doorframe,
    Hesitant to go in.
Scared of what I'd find.
But I continued into the room
    of hidden things
      Shrouded in mist.

      Are you there?

I am drawn to ghosts.
I am a stranger, leaning
Against the doorframe,
    Wanting to know
    Wanting you to know
I love you.

MOTHER'S WAY

1.

I feared you would say,
"Stop annoying me. Go away!"
    I wanted to be near you.
So I stayed inside in pajamas
On summer schoolfree mornings
    Of cool shallow breezes.

I was little—six or seven.
    Our windows gave closely on the sidewalk.
I looked out from our
    first-floor small apartment,
Other kids called up to me,
    "Come out and play."
Their boundless energy poised
    on a summer moment,
Beckoning to the yellow-green hill
    of our early childhood
While dark woods tantalized
    from a close distance—forbidding.

Country in the city-town of
    workingclass Woodhaven.

My mother was busy—
    petite womanly housewife
     dusting, washing, cooking—
    Determined.
Heavy-footed apparition in an apron—
    Just out of touch.

"I never saw a kid who lounged the way you do!"

I pulled my dark, straight-haired head back inside.
Drawn to her, even though her attention was not easy,
   the quick reprimand was.

I wanted to be alone with you. But you liked
the *"girl with flaxen hair" and blue eyes.

Yet, you and your love were quiet, solid.
Not always within reach. But there.

   When you'd tickle me
   Like a pouncing cat
   While I stayed undercover
   Before I got out of bed.
   That was such fun—
   Grown-up controlled fun.
   Often better than kid-fun
     That could run wild, turn cruel.

When we'd go shopping together
   for food in the afternoon,
You'd say, "Let's go to 'The Avenue.'"
   Local street of stores
   Topped by rickety railroad flats
   Cut through by the steel-girded Jamaica El.
As a district of streetwalkers cutting through
   a grid of well-groomed residences.

I walked near you—the stylish lady
   Who went food shopping in three-inch spiked
heels, straight skirt and always a hat—
   Handiwork of your milliner's trade.

---

*The Girl with Flaxen Hair," translated from French *A Prelude* by Claude Debussy

We were Mother and Child
    Bonded forever.

When I was thirteen and afraid of life
and death I was walking with you
in Alexander's Queens department store.
    I sensed something wrong.
Something unidsclosed and undeparting.
You had found a lump in your breast.

While you were in the hospital
I thought I too had a lump;
After all, weren't we a unit?
And made my breasts sore
    in search of it
Like self-fulfilling prophecy.

The tacit nature of your mother love
    was never enough.
I wanted to be your fair-haired girl.
But you called me impractical,
    a dreamer, booksmart
      with no common sense.

        2.

Years later, I stood half-naked
    in the doorway—
The same doorway I imagined
"The Thing" of the '50s looming
When I was seven, in bed for the night,
    and trembling, wide awake and
      unsoothable—
The doorway of the room where you lay

      in half darkness.
I dreamed of you
        shapely, with small waist
   in a black taffeta cocktail dress.
You knocked at my window
   in pouring rain   on the fire escape,
   out of reach, but there.
I don't remember letting you in.
        Did you see me?

Now that I'm grown
I sometimes think of our cramped apartment,
   inhabited by strangers. (now?)
It doesn't seem right.
Shouldn't it always belong to US?
All those mundane events, family crises
   Personalities projecting—
Don't they imbue the lifeless material
   of rooms with essences? Essences
     that might extrude from walls and floors
Intrude upon other's lives?

I now live in another part
Of the city,
   In my apartment—alone,
Filling all spaces with Things.
Afraid if I don't
       Corpses might fill them.

You're gone forever.
And now I am drawn
   to ghosts.
Can you see me?
I think of you often.
Maybe you are now

Residing in your proper plane.
 I am a stranger
Leaning against the doorframe,
    Wanting to know
    Wanting you to know
I love you.

MISSING 1

Never fully appreciated
   Not fully grieved
       Obliquely revered.

Time's refractions
   change perceptions.

Distance warps.
Absence grinds
   the mind-warped extraneous
      to dust.

Essence remains—
   Ghostly core,
      Love wallows in.

MISSING 2

Never fully appreciated
Distance changes remains.
In absence you love fully.
Ghosts wallow in refracted essence.
The extraneous erodes.
Not thinking warps grief.
Thinking warps grief.
Time obliquely warped
Grinds revered core.

A CHILD'S DREAM

I was about seven.
I was naked
My mother held my waist.
   My skin began
     breaking apart.
It was so thin
My insides were oozing out—
   my ketchup insides.
My skin was opening—
   all over.
A new split developed—
Moment by moment.
Helpless.   Bursting.
All that thick, red stuff.
My essence
   seeping out
     through wide cracks.

"VERY EARLY IN LIFE IT WAS TOO LATE."
—Marguerite Duras, *The Lover*

A foul vapor
       lurked
in the hallways
in the bedroom.

I dreamed
I, made of catsup,
broke apart
oozing red
    thickness.

I stared silent. Across
the sick room
My sister

    convulsed.

Father hysterical
Standing over.
My mother always with
    outward calm
made warm
milk walked
me about
to quell
Panic—panic,
       a leopard
on the ready.

I prayed one night
    on my knees
    at my bedside,
    body swaying.
My sister called it,
    "weird incantations."

    Hold my breath!
    It could come
    anytime.

    From Destiny,
    To Pitiful family.

She died in February
    at 27.
I was in high school,
I remained silent.
The winter wore on.

MY INHERITANCE

The seed that burst
into wildflower junk
got a stranglehold.

Clutter is my company,
my comfort, my compulsion.
Oppressive, alive.

"Let life's detritus
proliferate, go forth
and destroy all spaces
    or
Corpses will fill them."

SEASONS;
SEASONS WITHIN

Autumn

IN AUTUMN

Chilled gusts encircle
medieval turrets and
carry ghosts in rust and gold
on a Fall day
in old New York.

My vision captured by fine sculpted detail
on ruddy brownstone townhouses.

Magical faces appear
from intertwined acanthus scrolls
and Celtic symbols twist
with ancient secrets.

I am gripped by something—
unknown
I like it
though it forebodes.

Time, the thief
nudges in gusts
an *intimation
of mortality
in a sudden overhead
swirl of rusty leaves.
But art in stone
vibrates to city life.
And pleased, I walk on.

* reference to "Intimations of Immortality" by William Wordsworth

IN AUTUMN 2

As the wind shoved me
along the street,
something flew at my lips.
I thought it was a leaf.
It was a monarch butterfly.

I, gripped by hopeless pity,
watched as the fragile being,
blown as a crumpled leaf
tumbled away—
    diverted
from its determination
to migrate south
for the winter
rather, perhaps
    into oblivion.

As the inexorable force
pushed with such ease
I felt kinship
with the rest of life.

Someone I met along the way
said I had been kissed by God.

A WALK IN CENTRAL PARK: AUTUMN

I walk under the huge whirling pergola
Of yellow elm, spiky oak and flames of
Maple smoked by a November sky.

Gusts are redolent of my dusky love
Who hovers in shivering leaves
Off the wood's edge.
Where is he now?
And a friend who is a friend no more.
Where is she?
She was always a bit strange.

Wild breezes sum up spirits
That became ashy casualties.
Ashes again dissolve into tannin
Ground litter kicked up by white throats
In search of food
Who eye me warily as I pass.

I go on undaunted, lock eyes with a
Squirrel who hopes for a morsel
He easily senses I don't have
And turns away.

Stung, I cross the park
Creating quick melancholy
In the wake of stirred leaves.

Winter

CHRISTMAS CLEAR

Wandering the mountain edge of cold blue crystal
    in a black velvet winter night,
Blinking brings red green yellow blue gleaming
Starlights with Northern centers that bleed
Bright in the black air.

I watch quaint Germanic cottages create a
Christmas hamlet.
In the valley of my mind's eye
Fat children lie in comfort under heavy quilts
    on old trundle beds.

Gently wolfen, I sniff the chilled air.
Smells of warmth—baked apple
    Buttery streusel—drift outside.

Moon white snow surrounds the houses
    Caressing fluff, not frozen water
    That flattens into black leaden layers
    of January's stagnant landscape.

Warmth is happiness fleeting
    But I'm not lost.
I'm in the house of spirits—protected
By human aurora borealis as
The gothic cold north star sky
Reflects the star of Bethlehem.

FROM THE METRO NORTH HUDSON LINE IN WINTER

From the train window
Passing layers of landscape
Carry me into stark, hueless
Beauty.

Design reduced—
A modern painting in dry brush
On clean white canvas.

A hardened river with barren bank
As stately Palisades rise
Spectral

Sometimes partly hidden—
A screen of trees
Whose dark network,
Sharp-angled branches—
A roughly-made lady's veil—
A lacy attempt to conceal
Frigidity.

I am the artist
Who pulls unseen golden threads
Through hardened strips
Of Earth skin.

BLACK ICE

I stare out
    the window of Metro North Hudson.

The train rambles along
river's edge in the Winter's night.

Palpable black
    fills my face.

Far off bright dots
Outline a lonely stretch of bridge,

Show sporadic dwellings;
Cluster densely for a town.

Fears arise—spontaneous
in wordless   sightless
Black

Whose viscous pitch
Could suck me
    through the window
Absorb me
    in the dimension
        of oblivion.

The moon remains
    an orb of silence.

In ancient memory
In the reptilian brain

Deep night pervades.
Predators stalk.
We, with no night vision
   band together,

Against the nocturnal foe
Who ambush
   kill swiftly
   without gesture
   without sound
   without pity.

Spring

LIFE FORCE

I ride past desolate trees, tangled vines
Drab brown in Early Spring.
Dead to the eye, but an internal life-flow
Quickens in anticipation of yellow-green newness.

Childhood days play hide-n-seek
Among the twisty wood interplay
My tendrilled desires reach into,
Search the sepia woods—they are unmoving.

My soul harkens back to the tree in the meadow,
The pond over the hill—
Smelly with life,

Where we kids delighted in discovering
Gifts of ancient stagnant water—
Tadpoles, catfish, turtles whose strange
Movements and features excited us

As we felt an undefined visceral connection.

We walked gnarled pathways in thorny
Mysterious woods, yet revealing lovely dogwood,
Wild blackberries, sweet honeysuckle
Whose tips we pinched and tasted.

We were the ragamuffins of the forest
Revelling in grimy, vibrant Life-force.

Summer

I AM SUMMER

Jasmine heat
Inside and out
Humid, healing heat
Inside, out,
    All around.

The jasmine swell
Softly sweats its essence.
Enters everywhere.
Enters me.

I recline in blossoms
Retreating from the world
A garland 'round my head.
Breathing, sweating, living
    Summer—
Jasmine, my protector.
Summer, my shaman.

CALL

Locusts celebrate the season of life
In the quickening cadence
Of their climactic song.

Samba sung by purring voices from
the Amazon-land of Always-Summer
Wafts on radio waves
    through balmy breezes that
Brush Balinese wind-bells into
    a mellow tinkle chime.

In the near distance
    the Staten Island ferry's
Sweet blasts sounding city people's
Sojourns in not-so-far-away places
With familiar-sounding names
    but
Fantasy rises in me with
the soft, estuarial swell.
Fantasy that would fly me
Out my ancient window—
    singing of Summer.

TRANQUILITY

Under the porch overhang
    that gives shade as
A benign summer cloud,
I am cloistered in
Foliage and low fences
Given negative space—
Background by a cloudless blue.

Liquid ribbons of bird songs
Ripple the pool of summer air.
A transporting breeze slowly
Envelops me with amniotic
                            fluidity.

I smell the sea air carried
    from a nearby beach
With scent of salt and life.
    I hear silence.
I stay serene in
            blue-green silence.

ESSENCE

Sitting
    on the back porch
    in the country

Surrounded
    by rich, silent green

Liquid ribbons
    of thrush songs

Ripple
    the pool of summer air.
    And I hear silence,

Silence.
    only soft wind,
    wind chimes

And silence—
        serene blue
            silence.

THE GIFT

City and nature—
a shimmering, unified phantasm
Immerses us in perfect excesses—
mellow, vibrant, loud, sweltering—
    Life at peak—
    It's Summer!

A pungent, but pleasant, earth smell
infuses clear air—
akin to a damp, musty cellar
Whose old, prized things send out
a scented greeting
to their familiars
as they descend the stairs
in search of something.
    The search goes on.

Sticky viscous heat enfolds us,
often overwhelms even thermophiles
who then seek ancient waters
for relief—from Summer.

Walk casually, but alertly
to receive offerings of local gardens
Whose dazzling hues—
cerulean, fuchsia, royal purple, sun-orange
swell into a bushy fragrance-melange
that dizzies mind and body—
    in Summer.

Urban noises become more
vivid, intrusive
amplified in moistened sound waves.

A child wails in the distance
The street vibrates in sympathy.

Inexorably driven to procreate,
insects who arrive only in
    high summer
send out "shushing" calls to
    procure mates,
unseen in the lush spread
    of branches.

It's all high art that
engages the senses.

When life is at peak
Death has no entrance
The bell will not toll,
Don't listen for it—
    It's Summer!

SUMMER LAZE

I long
     I crave
          I lounge

Song wisps warmly enter
    Through my windows
        All open   come in
   Mingle with me   although
I may not move
       Curved by heat
And laziness across my chair.
       Arms and legs bare
          In cotton shorts and silk camisole.

Sweat emerges suddenly   envelops my skin
        In a fine veil of glitter
   As silky straps slip
       Down my shoulders
  And I tingle
     As if touched by
         A shy lover.

A TIME

As I lie on my day bed
Humid summer air
Laden with soil and flower scents
Carries sun-still images,
Childhood moments on near-country sidewalks
Across from the woods of Forest Park.

We stayed outside all day
In full sweat and thrust
   of youth's play
Relentlessly in motion

It was Summer!
Easy, schoolfree domain of the young.
We played midst the white noise
   of overheated nature
Ourselves overheated in energy's
   aimless urgency.

White noise of innocent bees hum
Visiting seductive blossoms.
White noise of delicate mosquito
buzz searching for emanations
   of body warmth.

Caterpillars, ugly larvae of mature beauty
   appeared sporadically.
We excitedly stomped them
To hear their gut-squish
To see revolting ooze.

Not aware or not caring
Of an instance of future beauty
In an instant forever lost.
We as all young animals
Directed by Nature
Pursued play's aimless urgency
Until dusk and dinner.

FROM MY INSIDE JUNGLE IN SUMMER

Someone creates jazz-caribe-fusion on steel
        drums in the distance.

I from my open room
Watch small birds
With fiery head feathers
Chirp for black sunflower seeds
To feed begging fledglings—
Downy young from fertile
Spring couplings.

A humid fragrance from Summer's soil
Foliage floods my room,
Makes seeds soften and sprout,
Makes my hair unruly, full, frizzy.

The music and summer air
Carry me to memory life.

I run on the meadow hill of childhood—
Through smooth, short grass
Spotted wildly yellow
By buttercups and dandelions.

I run past high hedges
Heavy with tiny white clustered flowers
        that
Release earthy ancient fragrance
        in Summer's heat.

I run under cloudless endless blue.
I run in endless heat.

I stay in endless run.
I may not return,
I follow primal call of Earth.

NEVER TOO MUCH

Summer's deep green
Comes full thick circle.
Vine tendrils unable to
Contain choke one another
Creeping climbing over walls
In tropical New York.

I will wear hibiscus blossoms
Sense jasmine
Watch for birds of paradise
As I turn corners
Beneath full blast Sun.

Air is heavy
With moisture and grass smell
And Heat.

Heat that goes in me
Out of me Around
Sapping   Sucking energy
    Unrelenting
    Procreative.

At first it stalks—
Not fully sensed.
Then pounces
Whoosh, its cougar weight
    Overtakes.

Life flourishes in excess.

Animal young
Springborn wet and scrawny
Grow fat.

I move in my city habitat,
Hair damp and frizzed.
A lioness in top form—
Pulled by biological destiny.

A wild orchid
Opens shamelessly
For butterflies, bees
Any taker to enter, taste
And be brushed with
The dusty germ
       for new Life.
I wrap myself in pastel gauze.

I Am.
Hot with color.
Sweetly swollen
Ready to pluck.
I hang heavy
Feeling the fullness
   of Summer.

My body exudes moisture
Trying to cool itself.

I am an earth creature
Rising
Strong from rich topsoil.
Pleased carrier of organic fragrances.

Running a finger down my nose
I find it greasy with life
As I move languidly
At the top of the season.
Aware, so aware
   And tingling.

SHORTER POEMS
AND MUSINGS

Varied

1.
I am a child in a wooded haven
Brushing past high hedges
With tiny white clustered flowers
Emanating an earthy Jurassic scent.

2.
I, the tattered butterfly
You the pupa—becoming
I dream of frayed wings
Brushing the delicate elongated body
Yielding to kindred touch.

3.
Chubby orange pumpkin
Dusky blue grapes
Fat, red tomato
Plump lemons—
Hopeful healthful
    Swellings of nature
In a world of toxicity
        and techno grit.

4. Seeding

The seed that burst
into wildflower junk
Got a stranglehold
Clutter is my company.

5. Pansies

Evolved mini-lions
Transformed into
A tiny quiet state
Rendering neutral the predator
But leaving behind
    his alertness.

6. Wooly bear wind

Throws itself
    against my room's window
While I startled
        by aggression
        go further under cover.

7. The Child

Slim as a walking stick
Imaginative as a dreamer
Dreamy as a poet.

Fragile as a spider nymph
 running for cover at
  a breath of movement.

Sensitive as a small worm
   heaved up from heavy rain
   recoiling from a faint touch.

8.
Arboreal bones scoured
Ashen by relentless forces,
Haphazardly criss-cross
High terrain Montana.
Still secret lives over
Agitate mobile beings'
Collective unconscious in passing.

9. "Ity" Ditty

I got lost once in total insecurity.
I felt I'd shrivel into obscurity.
Bleak futurity oppressed me.
But Life's drift, chance occurrences
In interaction with my individuality
Brought me from immaturity
Into some authority.
Now I'm found.

10. Search

In the locker room
    empty of bodies
I called "Barbara"—
    No answer.
I rounded the bend,
    A wide-eyed young woman appeared
Then retreated
    into the shadows.

11.
The girl with
        Flying black hair
        Whipped wet across her face,
    Its earthly origins
      Reflected in ancient puddles.

For a fleeting moment
I understand
The necessity of flesh.

12.
Nature puts a stop to
the sensual excesses of summer.
"All good things must come to an end."
And this they do in the exquisite
Flamboyance of Fall.

13.
A tall sturdy tree is cut down
    by the wind—snapped in its prime.
Its head hits the pavement
Flooding it with deep russet
    luxuriance—
Never to appear on its being again.

14.
A "rescued" monarch butterfly
Clings to a pumice stone
    On an indoor ledge.
I watch it feed, excrete,
    Gradually die. Did it anguish?
Only those belonging to the
    Species-on-the-edge
    Show a capricious compassion.
"Nature shows no mercy to individuals."

15. **On the Death of My Guinea Pig**

Through the ambient noise of
radio and T.V., the deadening
silence grips my heart.
The living foliage
surrounding his tank transform
into a motionless, brittle
frame for its emptiness.

16.
The cool flames of Autumn
    Inspire our fascination with Fire
    Without fear of being burned.

Fall's cool flames ignite the fire
    Of Summer's funeral pyre.

17.
I saw a robin and was so
very glad. For I feared it had
not fared well in this slowly forming
hell with all the world in it—
as well as its creator—

That promising species gone
Sadly mad, taking the world
        down with it.

18. PRIVATE MUSIC

    When the rain started
I closed the windows,
Felt the greyness
Liked being inside
Looked forward to the sound
    Enjoyed being closed in like
                      a hermit
        Very calm
                With private music.

Dated Angst Years

19.   *February, 1975*
I drank in the beauty of a
perfect June day in deep drafts
    in a silent toast to Life.
Life is a fragile image
tenuously poised on a point of Time.

20. **Aftermath/Prelude**   *June, 1967*

Air hushed and thick
Laying over a bleakly
Sunny landscape
             unchanging
Frozen in a fear of
             impending storm.

21.   *September, 1969*
<u>Love</u> seems to be a function of
personality aberration.
It often seems to be conceived
randomly and maintained by Inertia.

22. *September, 1969*
The shadowy organism of my feelings
Moves erratically through chinks in reality.

My spirit rejects a fresh flow of reality
With a faultless immunology.

23. *December, 1969*
An unrelenting expanse of ocean
    glistering
Sinister under the sub-violet glare
               of a cloudy day.

24. *January, 1969*
Winter afternoon's oblique alabaster
light pervades but keeps its distance
with callous ascendancy—

As a man who loves and comes
masterfully, coldly leaving a nostalgia
for something elliptically felt, ever elusive.

I am assimilated with Winter's
              thin white light.

25. *January, 1967*

I distrust people who always verbalize
and analyze other people's feelings and actions.
They think words can substitute for their
feelings as the catalyst for creating bonds
between people. They also tend to word-build
an imaginary individual which they impose
as themselves.

26. **Obsession** *March, 1967*

A giant, sharply defined looming
up menacingly from a calm
    generalized environment—
Out of proportion, out of perspective.

A mutated offspring from
the marriage of Mind and Reality.

An image cutting across the planes of the mind
        instead
of resting within its own.

27. **An Essence** *February, 1969*

Distilled from the life-grind
    of self's diverse matter
Issues upward softly,
Forms an aromatic vapor—
    Strong, immutable—You.

28.   *September, 1968*
My spirit secretes a coating that absorbs
what you generate instead of protecting...

Don't touch me or I'll burn.
Don't touch me or I'll freeze—in pain—

Self-punishment inextricably blended with
self-protection.

29.   *March, 1968*
Beyond the sheer rock of immediate Being
lies a chasm of unknown quantities...

Each person is an amorphous universe
projecting endlessly—

A landscape of infinity into which
one may enter as matter
passing through matter.

30.   *March, 1970*
A depthless pit of troubled, viscous fluid
assimilates everything near
into its own stuff.

31. Chill *April, 1970*

Spring fills asphalt canyons
    with a chilled umbra of
        bright grey-green.

Estranged off-yellow shafts
    expose themselves moodily.

An uneasy mix of light and shadow
    briefly emerges.

*I wander brittle on a cloud.

---

* reference to *I Wandered Lonely As a Cloud* by William Wordsworth

Haikus

1.
Sallow, slivered moon,
Captured in sky's endless sweep.
Positioned by Fate.

2.
Young and healthy weed,
Growing in cracks of hardness
Asserts its being.

3.
A lone sick pigeon
On a branch rustled by wind
Pity pierced my heart.

4. Silence

Morning's white canvas
Brushed only by the ship's blast,
The caw of the crow.

5. Tears

Layered sediments
of Life's memories upheaved
in cleansing waters.

6. Insecurity/ Self-doubt

Spindly pallid hands
Climb and clutch with clammy touch
The unfolding rose.

7. The Mouse

Tiny creature lay
Gently in my flowerpot—
Final resting place.

MIXED THEMES

Homescapes: Apartment, Street, City

ELEPHANT EAR

My large elephant ear plant just birthed a
tender leaf. Yellow-green, Spring green.
Not the cool deep green of its mature siblings.
Very sweet, floppy but with sturdy, thick stem.
Pushing relentlessly toward the light.

I feel the one flat side of the stem cylinder
So characteristic of its clan as I caress
the new member of the family and tell her
how lovely she is. How happy I am to
welcome her to my living room. (Living
in the truest way.) Which I am little by little
trying to transform into a personal forest
where even non-pestilential plant fauna may
reside.

MOURNING CLOAK BUTTERFLY

On an Autumn afternoon
I hurried along ugly Atlantic Avenue
seeking quick refuge from the racket
of traffic and commerce.

Descending elephant clouds pressed
dusk onto the cold street. Suddenly
a familiar shape formed in my eye
on the rough pavement. A thin life
line on lifeless ground.

A butterfly here now?

Summer's creature, wing-tattered
masterwork of Nature off
migratory course? Escaped from
a vivarium's humid cloister?
A mourning cloak!

It's supposed to hibernate.
Everything to its season.

The butterfly within sprang forth.
Faceless lumpen street humanity
vanished.
I bent over faded yet
velvety brown wings
with faint blue dots edged
in frayed antique white.

I reached out to this image of
grace. It climbed upon my finger.

It needs nectar. But where?
Nature is shutting down.

I whisked it away to my—
our refuge.

Watched with hope
as the slender proboscis slowly
uncoiled into the sugar-water
I placed before it.

Will it gain strength? It drank
endlessly yet remained unmoving.
I brushed its leg; it flinched a bit.
I let it be. Evening had arrived.

Next morning I rose in
hopeful anticipation.
Still motionless the posture
had changed. The signs were there.
Life was ebbing.

Legs splayed then folded
back against its abdomen.
It listed.

The end had come—maybe
it's natural time

I did what I could.
Gave it warmth, nourishment.
I am glad.
I will not don my mourning cloak.
The butterfly is so vibrant.

SUNSET/ DUSK FROM MY ROOF

As I gaze at the Sun's blood
Weakening at close of day
I still see its power.
It diffuses in blue-gray sky
Creates streaks of coral—
Reluctant to go.

OUR lights now glitter, gleam
Shimmer in monster, majestic
Edifices asserting reason,
Pride and cleverness.
As the sky deepens they soon
Dissolve into whimsical kingdom of castles
    and palaces
That create longing for Timbuktu
Or Tulum in Quintana Roo.

The Sun still gently commands
With seductive pastel wisps.
The almost full moon keeps
Watch with bogus authority
As the magical kingdom now
Dominates the sphere
As it fades in with the
        Sun's fade out.

MY STREET'S LINDEN TREE

The linden tree
    bearer of beautiful fragrance
    bends its boughs of lush leaves
        as to embrace.
Chooses my path home—
    so I pass under its nurturing pergola—
        A protective mother—
        May be my mother.

I caress low-hanging leaves,
    say aloud, "You are beautiful,"
    as my mother in green, tender youth.

Winged seed pods will emerge next—
    ready for new-life flight.
Then, the delicate flowering
that carries a godly scent
that holds secrets of survival,
Sadly short-lived as all
        of life's flowering.

I recall a friend's words:
    "Too pretty to last."

A gift to our poetic instinct—our nature,
    though Nature rarely has us in mind.

Shortly thereafter the season will change.
Trees will draw in upon themselves.
Be reclusive as my shy mother
Saddened by Life and Death.

THE CITY

Sunshafts slant down,
Spread wide angle, garish
From soft pacific blue
Onto concrete flats.

Stopped only by
   Strong-box habitats.

And cast heat. Heat like
Equator heat
That strikes ungainly characters
Who pass silently within;

Who bear great burdens
   And cast long shadows
     That offer no relief.

CITY LINES

Man-made cubist constructs
    Slowly silently rise
    From the eye's mind.

Testaments to human fondness
For straight lines and right angles.

Solid and stable facades
    On an unseen zigzag
    Of faultline

Impose peace on a point in time.

CITY LINES REVISED

But at this time,
    There is no peace.
Rectangular towers once rising
above all others
appearing timeless
    as the pyramids
In a moment came down
    by the will of perverted men,
Causing a stinking ruinous
    depression in the earth,
    a fathomless crater
        In our souls.

HUMAN-MADE

Steel swoosh of Brooklyn Bridge
Overtakes the river and
Encounters rhapsody-in-steel/blue skyline
As aged brown water waves
Flows, laps, swishes in its bed
   and allows itself
To be pushed around violently
   from time to time
By man-made moving contraptions.

Tall man-constructs oversee
    Upright and Still
Impose on the view. Silently.
While their insides are
Rifled and rattled by human concerns.

Outside—
   Serenity: Deception.
Accompanied by Machinery's directed drone.
Blaring. Persistent. Constant.
Not like Nature's alternating current.
   Yet   a mirror of it.
   But   outdoing it.
Eventually, this may not be permitted.

*An aware friend in high school once said,
"Sunshine creates so much superficial happiness."*

* "FAR FROM THE MADDING CROWD"

The neighborhood is quiet.
I, in my bedroom cocoon,
    Lulled by a soft ambient hum
Jarred awake (a dog barks in the street)
From semi-somnabulance, aware
Of a raucous world out there.

My apartment, my hermitage
Secures me from "the madding crowd"—
Anonymous humans passing
On city commons
Interfacing with gadgets only
    Or rudely brush me bump me
    With or without gadgets
Not move a centimeter
As if resentful—
We have to share Our space?

**Far From the Madding Crowd* novel by Thomas Hardy

MY STREET IN PROGRESS

1.

Boulders from ancient upheavals
of infernal subduction zones—
    Quarried by humans
To make broad old slate sidewalks
That inlay my street
   in an odd grid
of smooth stone segments
Whose soft blue-gray
   dappled in sunlight
    rippling in shades of leaves
Refresh and complement
   the city walker
Past lacy curtains
   and
the thrill of flowers
That adorn pinkstone brownstones.

My street—
   arbored walkway—
    once cobblestoned—
of Victorian grace.

2.

My eye is drawn down
   to time-cut intaglio—
Block art in street time.
As my step proceeds toward
   my street's vanishing point
My vision is brought up short
   by downtown backdrop
    straight lines and angles—

Structures rise up in linear time.

Pink mimosa petals
   drop wantonly
     against stone slabs.
Then vanish as the period
   vanishes
Before the current world's
   rigid monuments—
Silent, stately,
   invade, hold captives,
Lock out the living—
Flowers, trees, birds, people.

People on the street—
Faceless no-name bulks
Get in each other's way.
Get in MY way.

     3.
A sagging old dump—
   a woman rocking
    from side to side
In rumpled dress
   battered slippers,
Barely hanging on to feet
Shuffling from bad legs
   and body weight—
A hull ready to sink;
Sunken lips from missing teeth—
Maybe a beauty
   of a time long gone.

I made an arc around
   her bulk and came

    Face to face with a sleek,
        too-thin young woman.

I was made to step aside
    Not to be struck
By her determined gait
That carried her in unswerving
    Linearity intent on her cell.

A natty lawyer glanced her way—
    Mating in his desires—
Doing the defense dance
    for the indefensible
Through the grid of male logic.

        4.
I stepped into my block's
    healthfood store.
As I was stacking up on food
    uncontaminated by industry,
I witnessed a young mother
    pleading with her toddler
    to sit in the stroller
Laden in back with bundles.
She dared not command the child,
    for fear of…
The stroller crashed backward
As the youngster bolted
      down the aisle.
The obvious escaped the mother.
I wanted to say I could have
    predicted that. I didn't.
I paid and went back onto my block.

Oh, deliver me from
    Dusty vapor breath
Rotten flesh
    Common sense deficit

Denial of putrefaction,
Animal instincts and Death.

Always Death—
        behind conversations
        over wireless phones
Sometimes said to cause brain tumors.

Death—darkest thread running
        through Life's fabric.

The beautiful lifeless
    Stones bear witness
To Life's inexorable progression
        On my street.

MY STREET IN PROGRESS II

        1.

Ah, the birds
I love the birds.
Local breaths of spirit.

As I walk
I watch pigeons stroll,
 Sparrows hop, starlings swagger
   with facility in our midst.
I look for the robin or mockingbird
   on the way to less crowded locales.

In constant search for food
   They deftly avoid heavy human
   steps. Create a lyrical ambience.
   Hardly noticed by most
   On their hurried way.

Squabble over mates, territory—
Seldom to the death.
Bring up helpless young
   in the human ruckus.

        2.

A soft gray newly fledged
   starling jumps away from
   oncoming cars.
Sends out throaty distress calls;
Caring parents call back.
The baby runs to take cover
   under a parked car.
I, not surprised if the parents
   told their baby;

Consider me a possible menace.
   eye me, size me up.
   I pass too close.
   they fly away.
I admire the straightforward
   Diligence; simple intelligence.

In Spring the human alarm
   goes out as heated but wary
   chatter among neighbors:
"The neighborhood birds have
   commandeered our air conditioners
   for their nests."

Nests cleverly created—
   an impacted mound—
   dry grass, twigs, feathers,
   lottery ticket scraps.
The machines whirr and do nothing.

       3.
Resourceful wild creatures
   Stop the machines
   that give creature comfort;
   rattle our quotidian existence,
While we become inured
   in video and print
To bare-boned visages—beaten,
   diseased, starving in
   continual outbreaks of carnage,
   torrential blood-letting.

Something is off-balance
   on my lovely street.
   Ah, but the birds.
   I love the birds.

STREET FEAST

A crowd's steady-state talk-noise,
    Unbroken tone density
Issues as from a single living entity.
The ramblings of an omnipresent street being.
But thoughts are light, faces relaxed—
    No density, no intensity of mood.
    No unity—only apparently.
The whole is greater than the sum
    Of its parts.

Food fragrances merge with sounds,
    Colors, stenches
Forming a pungent, raucous
    Gutty street thing
A rank, savory, joyful
    City offering
Unto the power-that-might-be.

MY HABITAT

I sit in my livingroom and realize I've created
a porch, a terrace—in effect, an outdoor area indoors
with my tall, spreading plants that shed leaves and
attract bugs as Nature—and I allow it.

I am the nature-loving authority here—
a benevolent ruler to living things.

In Summer I listen to the outside natural sounds—
windows flung open, no screens—like the
orgasmic swell in August heat and haze of locusts,
cicadas, crickets life-noise. I revel in it, for I
know in a few weeks it will vanish for a year.

I listen to rain against the windows and in any
place where it will make its sound, and think of it
as my private music.

Friends

SESTINA FOR MY FRIEND

She was my friend
And this week her life
Came to an end as all things
Do, whether or not we do nothing.
She wasn't that old—
Not for recent years.

We were friends of many years.
Sometimes I questioned, "friend"?
Maybe she's too old.
That's what's strange in life.
I really know nothing
About the true nature of things.

Today I saw all her things
Collected over the years
Strewn about; equally nothing.
What becomes of this friend?
What can I take away from this life?
An acceptance of getting sick, becoming old?

We all must get old,
Yet it is the most despised of all things
That are fixed in life.
It's a pity we don't value all our years
Before a friend
And her effects come to nothing.

We laughed over nothing
We didn't feel how old
Age can happen to a friend
We saw the absurd in things.
We didn't act our years
As they passed us in life.

How precious is life!
Yet we often reduce it to nothing
By loitering through years,
Forgetting we get old,
Fretting about material things
To the day we become that immaterial friend.

A friend is Life
And makes things from nothing.
But everything gets old and sees its expiration of years.

SILENCE

The snow falls straight
and delicate; so as not
to disturb,

My friend lies
trying to sleep
in the next room.
severely disquieted,
yet not disabled
by Parkinson's.

I gaze out the bay
window, mesmerized,
enveloped in the soft
gray of the day.
The pines are still
against the
whitened sky.

My mind connects
where there is no
connection, but
then who knows?

Nature
may be assisting
a sought quiet
for the world-weary.

Both I and my friend
have a calm moment,
in Idaho for a film
festival of the spirit.

We left the feature
last night. Fatigue and
malaise summoned a
soothing image—
the guest house
penetrated
our bonded consciousness.

I took her arm to help
her leave the theatre.
There were icy spots. We
waited in the cold for
the pick-up van.
She stopped, held
the lamppost. I waited.
She exclaimed with
exasperation, "Sometimes
I wish I could die!"
I protested in a knee-jerk,
"Don't say that!"
She pushed me away.
"You don't understand!"

The meaning of Life is the holy grail.
No more animal instincts. We're left
to personal mythologies.

"The tulips are too excitable, it is winter here." —Sylvia Plath

A VISIT

I went to see him in the nursing home,
    bright as a rainbow
    swollen with smell
Not prepared
    to stare straight
    into the face
    of decay.

                Where is the spirit
                        in beaten flesh?

Nurses scurried
    in official white
    to serve up
    business as usual.
My mind swooned.

My eyes rolled.
I took his hand,
    shook withering flesh,
His lips moved—
      knowing.
"Hello, Jim. It's Carol."

Cut flowers
    flanked the weary—
    arriving too early
    for the service.

Rotting fruit in every room.
Each softening into its own cup.
   Soon to be gathered
   To compost waiting earth.

                Where is the spirit
                    that must triumph, transcend?

ELEGY FOR ROSIE

We met in retired teachers' jazz.
We met again in French.
Synergy connected our humors
The ready children
    burst forth.
We became "les méchantes élèves"—
    the naughty pupils
Who talked and laughed too much.
    Teacher yelled at us.

When I walked into poetry
    After a few separated years
She gleefully shouted, 'My sister.'

Love of life and learning
    was her Muse.
She, the embodiment of
    a perfect marriage—
Childlike exuberance
for all facets of the jewel called Life
With a seasoned afficionado's
Appreciation of the richness
    of human creativity, and
Empathy, compassion for
Tragedies great and small.

She's gone now. We are left stunned.
As is we barely accept death. So
How do we accept someone so engaged
    with the world leaving it?
How does such vibrancy become non-being?
Her spirit will continue to vibrate the realms
    of the many she's touched.

ALIENS

Strange design
   Not of body—
      of mind.
Nervous impulses shoot out,
Strike, sometimes kill.
Not by plan
—by natural imperative.
To satisfy needs I only obliquely sense.

Someone named J. and I
   walked passed images in a gallery.
Were stopped short
   by cloths covering lovers' heads,
   a man-in-a-bowler's face
   masked by a smooth green apple,
   a large pipe with an inscription that
   insisted: "This is not a pipe."

We talked of art—
   that process of
Converting energy-to-matter
   feeling-into-form
  in tunes, words, hues
   only circuitously cerebral;
Striking squarely in the senses.

Our words carried images for mutual
   understanding—
We thought.
We probably guessed, and second-guessed.

J. seemed humble, sympathetic,
   down-to-earth.

We went to dinner.
She blew smoke in my face.
She had to.
Who the fuck is she?!

*"La belle dame sans merci!"

I imagined dying at the hand
   of a stranger.
She and her exhalation
   were permeating my known-being.
I left. I went home—contaminated.

E.—Friend for a quarter of a century,
Loves, accuses, castigates me, and
   most of the time isn't there.
Lives—a phantasm in my mind's-eye.
Materializes briefly after searching for me.
Fades out very soon.
Don't see eye-to-eye.
What do we see? We feel—
   an amorphous existence that
    breathes and feels
       What?

E., Young male who struggles and
   creates his own world
   admires me, thinks I'm a doer.
He doesn't really know.
Purloins pieces of my persona
   from time to time to sustain his.

Once a tape of me in his voice
switched on in conversation
about being on the same wavelength

La Belle Dame Sans Merci poem by John Keats

as kids. That's why we get along so
   well with them.

He doesn't deal with them—I do!

I'm older.
Experience has painstakingly built
   my life and spirit into their
present structure by subtle, gradual
accruals to the masonry—
     impenetrable.

The smash of a telephone receiver
  jars my sensibilities
    makes short shrift of my desires.

"You get angry for nothing," I say.
"It very much feels like something," he says.
I think: "It becomes something invasive
   and ugly for me."
"It's all part of your peculiar system."
   He becomes silent—
en route to his own galaxy.
Space travel is difficult and costly.
   Don't go!
      Let's dance.

Reality and fantasy
   slither and swirl
Copulate, separate in our
   liquid ballet.

Lovers

FANTASY ON "ROMEO AND JULIET"

Seeds of love—
  Often sequestered
      in forbidden fruit.

Fantasy love
   in liquid liaisons
      often fatal.

Overwhelming rush
Adrenalin gush
      into each other's arms.

Embrace in fantasy-woven web—
   Seems strong gossamer—
Really water silk
   Evaporating
Before love-struck eyes.

REFUGE

You—Me
    Us.
Are We?
Strong bonds.
    Of what?
Did we create US from
shadowy needs and
        desires—so often at odds?
Or are we an island
    thrown up from the interplay
        of self-forces,
Midst the world's erratic undulations?

We are a-shimmer
    as a heat mirage—
        Shapeless.
Details of our existence
    bleed and blur.
When the heat lifts,
    and the air clears
a small oddly-configured land mass
        appears.
A harsh place with precipitous outcroppings
            of rock
That lead to the sea
    Inhabitants unknown.

FAVORITE LOVER

     1.

His voluptuous lovemaking
   Expresses his
   Lush body
   Lush soul.

As I move my hands
   through
   touseled thick dark hair
   Fiery feeling moist eyes
   Engage my sloe-eyed
   expectant stare.

His slender smooth
Café creme body
Child-like   delicate almost,
Yet a supple, slithering
Python around me.

Our movements mingle
With words rising
   from depths
In the hushed equatorial air.

Earth-pungent fragrances
   Issuing from body recesses
     Mix
   With pleasure purrs.

Our bodies oddly rendered incorporeal,
   We rise up
   My room—an amniotic blurr.

But—
    many years later

    2.
I forgot his name. No,
My senses lost an intense craving

For him.
I had to have.
Had to possess.
    Feared losing.
This creation of male beauty—
    Lushness of body
Ghostly illusion of soul.

I had to love urgently
    Passionately,
Forget the world
    But, I ached.

He was never mine.
Maybe never wanted him to be.
An *obscure object of desire.
A plaything of my mind.

Now
    He's a neutral memory
    Evoking nothing
    Only wonder at how
    Temporarily insane I was.

I didn't forget his name.
I never had access to it.

**That Obscure Object of Desire*, a film by Luis Buñuel

HEAT

He silently gazes—cool
with hooded
brown eyes.

I languidly feel the warmth
    of his smooth earthtoned body
Sprawling sleekly over my bed—
    unmoving.

Across from us
Lush green leaves
Hold themselves erect
From healthy bodies
    of house plants
Creating illusion
    of eternal Summer.

Our eyes and lips meet.
Outside fragrant air calls
    us to come
But allows us to stay
With gentle puffs
    of breezes which
      softly penetrate
      wooden lattices.
Mingling outside with inside.

> "And what is actual is actual only for one time
> And only for one place."
> — T.S. Eliot, from "Ash Wednesday"

HIM

I met him at my cousin's one Christmas
    in the country.
He was stringy, twenty with thoughtful air.
We were all in holiday mode.
Lights and colors a-shimmer.

Eyes met in instant attraction.
My cousin's daughter said,
    "He likes you."
I was hot in those days.
I was thrilled.

Through youth's awkwardness
I saw something hidden, pained;
A delicacy of demeanor, gesture.
A questioning—like me at that age.
    Extremely, tall, Black,
      Handsome with a hint of homely—
        a lazy eye, a bony face.

I acted cool.
Quipped about his beanpole look;
Seemed carefree, in control—
Really anything but.

After that day I passed the word
    for him to call.
I yearned, obsessed.
He called and asked in a velvet voice

"What kind of erotica do you like?"
God, I wanted him.
He was elusive, unreachable then—
By phone, by feel.

2.

Time became telephone defined—
A teleyear passed,
Before we became lovers.

Life continued after passion—
    He moved in.
A pale moon washes his image clear now.

I can't forget his slender
Naked well-formed person
With sweet just-showered smell
Soft armpit hairs
Soft perspiration-scent up close
Moving from room to room
In freedom and grace.
Wearing only foam
animal print slippers.

3.

He was often not there
But we were close.
We talked, we felt everything—
Meaning of life, death, god;
Nobility of creatures,
How dogs know how to have fun
Better than humans.
    and then on-going disturbances.

He once found a cicada
    Inside buzzing, big, green.
    Captive.
We freed it together,
Laughing that it might
Backtrack and land on us.

I remember many walks—
We went feeling all the seasons
In controlled landscapes of city parks.
In the straight and narrow
    of concrete gridlock
Yet conducive to eruptions of temperament.

On our bridge—beautiful stone
Gothic Brooklyn.
We'd walk calmly
Oddly without conflict
In rarified air
    Turbulent current
        Still towers.

4.

He said it would be forever.
"You're my baby," he said.
Baby needs hugs.
He gave them readily.

Then he hid from the world.
    Resisted going out,
    Swaddled his long form
    in daytime sheets. Slept long.
    Couldn't cope. I couldn't cope.

Eventually he left
    By mutual understanding.
    He often said he didn't like Life.
    I cried hard.
    He went away to get a foothold—
    Some balance or an end to it.
    I mourned. I was relieved.

He once had written me a note
It said, "you are the single most
    important force of good in my life."
He said, "your love has made a man
    of me." "Loving you always."

Words, issues of a moment in Time.
In time it all changed.

5.

In Time and distance we drifted apart.
We are the past now—
    As the pale moon
    Washes his image clear.

REMEMBERED

Eric, Eric long gone.
I hear from you now and then—
Inspired by a deep pang of
Remembrance or
Impelled by memory flash
With little depth?

When we met your calls
Were erratic. My longing
Was all-consuming.
When your silence became
A heavy load I called you.
You were asleep in the afternoon.

Your depression was profound
Your disturbances a viscous tangle,
Yet your bearing had a silent intelligence,
A gentility I found irresistible.
You were that * "obscure object of desire"
Your mystique's power loosened living together
        three years.
Reality often invades the realm
of the imagination—the Great
Factor in Love's enthrall.

**That Obscure Object of Desire*, film by Luis Buñuel

9/11

THOUGHTS ON SEPT. 11

Out from murky depths
Of the evolutionary past
    Further obscured, but
Thinly veiled to seers
    by civilization—
Distracting trappings
    of rationality—
Come primal screams
    of chaos:
Fear Anger Hatred,
Primate calls
    of Revenge, Destruction,
From creatures volatile
    as the earth itself,
Spewing poison gases
    from their depths,
Corroding the chain-links
    of common humanity.

AFTER EFFECTS

I arise each morning in the comfort of my home,
Turn on the radio to stirring or soothing jazz—
While prolonging breakfast—my favorite meal
My favorite time of day—new beginning.
    The day—manageable time unit.
Yet in a layer of my mind knowing instability resides,
That life is laced with brutality.

COMMEMORATION DAY 9/11/02
PROLOGUE

We must deal with grief.
    What a terrible undertaking.
We're helpless.
We're mere mortals.
We have no choice,
We must deal with grief.

All day and from the start of the week, leading
up to it the John Donne lines: "Send not to ask for
whom the bell tolls, it tolls for thee," were
going round in my head.

SATURDAY, SEPTEMBER 14 · EPILOGUE

Real life is rank. Right now I'm at home in
my ratty pajamas with head cold misery.
I smell my armpits. I may as well be a goat.
I'm sweating from post-menopausal heat and the
day's high humidity.

My face is damp and mixed with the grease
of my Mediterranean ancestry.
My hair is an uncombed wild frizzed bulk.
I enjoy twirling it, feeling its robust yet soft wooly
texture, I like being an animal, but uneasily;
I can be wounded. Die, watch others die.
    Not knowing what comes next.

All Mixed

THREE WRITINGS FROM LINE QUOTES FROM "ASH WEDNESDAY" BY T.S. ELIOT

1.   *April, 1970*
"Against the word the unstill world still whirled."

Wandering worlds of piecemeal people
   half determined to make a whole
   through fractional affinities—
And, the jagged glass comes crashing through.

Wondering whirls of piecemeal people
determined toward infinity
But, there is no whole to <u>be</u> greater than its parts.

2.   *March, 1969*
"...And I who am here dissembled
proffer my deeds to oblivion, and my love
to the posterity of the desert..."

Lying, my arms extended—
      beseeching
My thoughts move freely,
   wildly, without bounds,
   rootless   wasted
My visitors are stone pillars.

3.   *October, 1969*
"Because I cannot drink
There, where trees flower, and springs flow, for there is
nothing again."

In a quiet spring meadow
an unseen but palpable
organic substance is formed
from the life-liquid
of trees, warm air water
combining. Solid.
Suddenly thrown splattered
scattered, thinned in the Wind—
      Gone?
Parts lose gravity for each other
   Matrix lost.

Rotting lion's teeth remain
   against the delicate pallor
      of an April hill.

Dedicated to Eleanor Comins, watercolor artist and teacher

STREAM OF CONSCIOUS, STREAM OF COLOR

I glide my brush
    across moistened textured paper
        as in a caress.
  My spirit flows
        in the wake of color,
   Vibrating in vividness
   causing a musical hum
        of contentment.

The brush moves
        as by its own volition.
   out of the mist seeps
     a red dusky spread
       of Autumn foliage.
then saturated blue and green branches—
  a ghostly emergence
        against a pallid pink sky.

As I glide my brush
    across finely textured paper
   moistened to readily receive
    but not control
        the color burst
     that would take over
        if not guided by the artist—
      who is only half-aware
         of the outcome,
While luxuriating
        in the sensual flow
   of paint across paper.

AT SIXTEEN

She gingerly told her boyfriend of the
Leaden ball of fear occupying her pit.
He showed annoyance; didn't want to hear
While they rode the precarious elevated train
That travelled on a wood slat trestle
With views of the river on each side
Over the Williamsburg Bridge.
She remained deceptively still even
In the stoney face of resistance and
Capricious danger; went
Further inside dreamily
But with dead bolt lock.

MIRRORS

Out of the womb
    and
    through the
        looking glass.
The first 18 months
    of Life—
An accelerated Drama
    of Learning.
Caregivers order,
Imposing their perspective.

Adolescents dramatically
Break the glass,
Repiece the shards
    of Self and Not-self.
Create a new image —
The perfect image of
    our mind's eye.
Our eyes smooth
    the rough edges.
Force a fit.

But beyond the sheer
creation of Immediate Being
Lies a chasm
    of unknown quantities.
Each person is an amorphous
universe projecting endlessly.
A reflection of infinity.
Into which one may enter
As energy passing through
    Matter.

In the search for Infinity
Optics are governed by
 the Laws of Physics.
We look.
We see desires and anti-desires.
We wander through
 the synergy of
 Reality and Illusion.
Where is What is?

ON THE BEACH

Slender alabaster
Asian statue
Delta of Venus, a polished pearl
Stands on the shore
      of the ages.

The China Sea polishes
alabaster and marble
to perfect a China doll.
      I want her.

An iridescent jade locust
chirps mockingly—
ancient signal of
      late summer.

I watch under a burnt
orange striated sky.
The alabaster doll,
caught by a wave, dissolves into salt
before my widening eyes.
Vanished far away
      or vanished forever.

A chill of fall passes.
My body absorbs it with a tremor.
The white caps break on the shore.
The gulls circle and call out.
The sea life moves farther out.
I return home, confused and hurt.

PALISADES

Gray clouds move vaporous waves
Midline in the smoky Palisades.

The river, kindred monotone expanse
Separates them from the living.

Humans need no color in
This world of Pleistocene upthrust.

*Non-human concretion outcrops sea fossils
As earth churns and rechurns
In unexpected directions, in lovely formations.

Eyes that outcrop the headrock gaze,
Longing toward the beauty in the rocky mist.

**Human Concretion*, sculpture by Jean Arp

MY BLOUSE

It's off-white.
It's loose.
It hangs unevenly.
It helps me transform.
I'm simpler,
    more innocent.
I'm a country girl
    in the city.

Then again,
Maybe it just
    hangs sloppily.
Maybe I am dishevelled.
It has the ambiguity
    of a casual
    yet personal
remark from a stranger.
No, I'm a country girl,
But in the city.

MYSTERIES

I wander ancient sand,
    Search secrets of primordial seas
        My spirit bathed in surf sound.
I pass a coconut in weathered husk.
    It holds a secret—
        An ancient journey taken long ago
            From an African birthplace,
        Carried on convulsive ocean currents,
        Seeding the New World with
            Tropical boughers-become icons.

A tiny lizard of vibrant animus
    Turns its head—looks up at me
Me—a potential danger. I am struck by
    the intelligent intent of
The miniscule creature's stare.

Embedded with sea shards, a
    Portuguese Man-of-War seems
        no more than a bloated blue plastic sac
            if not for an
    Array of slender tentacles.

Transparent, empty
    No internal organs, no Brain yet
part of a ½ billion-year-old
    Family secret of Mindless survival.

BUTTERFLY CONSERVATORY

I, there to protect
   airy wings
every week
   to inform
visitors   transported
   by
   flights
    of
      live art.

I killed Isabella Tiger.
   My unknowing foot
   imprinted
     pale
       striped tracery
   into the carpet.

Orange of its guts
matched orange
   in its wings,
   oozed from its abdomen
   as it lay
     in my palm.

I, there to inform and protect.

    The innocent kill.

    The innocent die.

        Harsh world.

COUNTRY ROAD

Heated silence is
An animal waiting,
In a bright grassy field
Given over to crowds
Of tiny pink and yellow
Wildflowers,
    and
In the dark intrigue of
Cool forest.

The silence beckons me,
    Primed with expectation
Of something eventful.

Though not on firm footing
I make my way
    Through white and black
    Local noise
    Toward primal silence.

REVERIE

    1.
I land on the shore
of a warm, shallow sea
whose tranquil waves
slush upon soft sands.

A primordial sea
formed from terrestrial cooling.
I follow a trail of
aromatic vapor in air
hushed and humid.

I am carried into a soothing
vortex of breezes
fragrant with cinnamon
and vanilla.

Let down in the surf
At low tide where
I am gently rocked.

I lose all sense
of Time and its events.
hours, days, months—
even years, perhaps.

I cruise, bask, dream
I revel in the moment
    moments stream.
    senses sated.
    mind at peace.

2.
In a moment
Waves climb higher
Get rougher.

I am caught in riptide
Washed away
Heaved back
Into the world.

I am once again
in familiar space/time.

Now walking midst
Surface beauty
   but
Armed against
   Surface tensions.

THOUGHTS ON HUMAN NATURE

LITANY AND RHYME TO HUMAN NATURE

We are:
    Naughty by nature
    Milky-kind by nature
    Brutal by nature
    Caring by nature
    Indifferent—
        We can't be bothered!

Self-serving by nature
Self-sacrificing by nature
Self-involved by nature
Self-destructive by nature
Self-righteous by nature
Self-deprecating by nature
Self-aggrandizing—
        Self is the key.

Defensive by nature
Expansive by nature
Larcenous by nature
Murderous—
        If only in thought.

Sympathetic by nature—
Judgmental by nature
Civilized by nature
Wild by nature
Extremist by nature
Middle of the road—
        But oblivious to traffic.

Artistic by nature
Practical by nature
Obtuse by nature
Clever—
    But not wise.

Logical by nature
Irrational by nature
Risk-taking by nature
Cowardly by nature
Moving and shaking
Inert—
    I hate change.

2.

Often delusional and usually dysfunctional—
    What a group!
From the ridiculous to the sublime.
Will we adjust in Time?

We don't get out of the kitchen
Even when we can't stand the heat.

We're hard pressed to 'use it,'
    Neither do we want to lose it.

We want our cake after eating it.
    We never learn from history
        And keep repeating it.

We do unto others exactly
    What was done unto us
        (Especially if it's bad.)

We behave in ways we hate
    Then we get mad
        (Usually at someone else)

We persist in acts done unto ourselves
    That will surely leave a scar.

We role-play with others like children
    And, like children, think it's real.

Hurting ourselves
    Getting a bruising
        At war with ourselves,
            Without doubt losing.

WE are the crowning glory of Creation?

Oh, God! That's UNreal.

DEAD END

We, the garbage generators
    dump black bags
    stuffed with un-civilized
    detritus everywhere.
    On the road to nowhere.

Nature has no garbage.

We, masters of the universe
    conquer all environments
    all creatures
    plant them firmly
    On the road to nowhere.

Nature's dynamic is the master.

We, arrogantly create a closed system
    to suit us and only us.
We, ignorantly snap our minds shut
    set Nature's perfectly calibrated
    balance of life
    On the road to nowhere.

Nature loves the circle—no loose ends.

We, imagine we have control,
We, are out of control,
    out of balance
    out of bounds
    out out out!

Nature will win out.

Men and nations behave wisely once they have exhausted all other options." — Abba Eban, former Israeli statesman

A JAUNDICED-EYE VIEW IN "COUPLETS" OF CONTRADICTION OF THE TRAGI-COMEDY OF BEING HUMAN
(with *comments* and *quotes*).

Despite frequent bathing in the delusional milk of human kindness,
Are we not more often animals — 'armed
    and extremely dangerous?'

Proponents of peace fiercely protest, pound pavements
    marching,
Ignoring an unbroken history of making war.

I fear we are an innately bellicose species.

Human male mammals paw the ground and lock horns,
Talk peace, work to make and then easily break treaties.

Our collective creative genius gives rise to myriad cultures and tongues.
Our ingenious technology brings us together; catastrophic clashes ensue.

We hold an ideal of universal brotherhood—
But instead, behold the stranger in our neighborhood,
'Get out!'

Fast-paced advances in technology, facilitated;
Hurling rocks in anger, facilitated;
    compromise, unfacilitated!

"A river is a boundary between two countries. On one side of the river, my friend; on the other side of the river someone I shall be praised for killing."
   —Blaise Pascal, French philosopher
      and mathematician, 17th century.

Some rescue June bugs.
Some strangle cats.

Some jump on train tracks to save a stranger.
Some rob life-savings of friends.

'We've got to rescue that buck stuck in the mud.'
'Next week let's hunt and shoot some deer.'

The unconscious mind can roil with inner conflict,
   hatred, self-hate.
Do not unto others as you do not want done to you...
   massacres trending.

Rare holy men have proposed:
   Do unto others as you would have them do unto you.
The more common bully illustrates,
   Inflict on others what we have and think we've suffered.

Why do we sometimes behave in ways we loathe in others—
An apparent innate disability for self-awareness.

"Some day my prince will come," however—
'I can't get enough of that cavalier, unreliable guy I met.'

"I'm a menace to myself." —a friend.

Blind self-interest can crush relationships, civilizations
— the world.
Through it all we tightly grasp
*"the thing with feathers."

Our consumer economy creates massive garbage
    defiling the Earth.
In natural ecology one living thing's waste is another's
    food. No garbage.

In nature all is calibrated for a perfect cycle of existence. Because we have created a world mainly for us alone, everything is thrown off-balance.

"*Man's normal condition is to be a misfit.*"
    —from "Uncle Vanya" by Anton Chekhov.

---

*"Hope is the thing with Feathers," poem by Emily Dickinson

ANTHROPOCENE

There are beings in my abode—
        One with graceful predator's gait,
  Once sleek hunter—
  Wildness a distant memory!
Now beloved companion
        Contentedly cared for,
        Castrated in captivity,
While many roam urban streets
        in search of discarded morsels.
Others rooted in green silence
Move to internal rhythms.
        Secret lives
        Language in code
        Codes not yet broken
        Unique genomes—
Some parts I share
Many swathed in mystery.

There are beings outside
  As a new year begins—
        Lives sacrificed to serve
        As glittery centerpieces
        For a great winter festival.
        Some still vibrantly green
Now carcasses left to molder
        On frigid concrete
        In crass positions
Showing no respect
        For elegant, complex lives
        Lived in secret
During the oblivious reign
Of Earth's dominant species.

PROSE PIECES

FOR PEOPLE WHO ARE AFRAID OF OTHERS AND THE THINGS OF THE WORLD
March, 1966

A perfect relationship: a formal attachment,
a desperate but empty closeness; calling each
other anxiously, seeing each other all the time—
but separate, made substantial by mutual need
to protect oneself from the outside world—
non-acceptance of another person within the bonds
of formal relationship.

A fallacy—each person crystallizes into a
microcosm of the outside world for the other.
The futility of a partnership in which each has
only self-defense to give makes the outside more
frightening in its representation through this
person—yet more appealing in contrast to the
negative intimacy of the tortured relationship

The person is a dichotomy—the world and security
from it. Both are unfairly invested in one person.
The world should be an arena whose benefits
would be the sources of satisfaction in an
intimacy which would in turn make the world
a rich experience.

My feelings are as anti-matter is to matter,
Self-punishment inextricably blended with
    self-protection. My spirit secretes a coating
That absorbs what you generate instead of protecting...

DRESSING WITH FEELING

I could easily sink into an abyss of nothingness from inertia. Everything is a project—even getting dressed. Sometimes I feel I just want to be left alone by the world which expects too much of me. Don't ask me to get dressed! Don't expect me to dust! It's an effort to remove my bathrobe, slip my nightshirt over my head. Feel the sweat under my breasts. (God, they're big!) Slide my night pants down. Step out of them. They will sometimes resist removal and stick to my legs before finally coming off. This makes me angry, and I let loose a string of invectives against the animus that causes clothes and inanimate objects of everyday life to come alive with intent to thwart my movements, my life! Then I choose a pair of socks high enough to provide warmth in Winter under my outside pants. But first I must put on my bra, harnessing my endowments.

I hook it around my upper abdomen and turn it around to the back, getting a slight friction burn. If I don't do it this way I'll get strained muscles, reaching behind to do it. Should I wear an undershirt? Yes, and put a fleece shirt over it—that wonderful, soft synthetic that blocks out aggressive breezes. Slide into my favorite shoes—U S Keds canvas mary janes. But they don't let me just slide in. I have to bend over and fit them and fasten the velcro straps. They have holes in the soles. I don't care. I love them. I'll never find everyday shoes like them again, so I'll deal with the effort it takes to bend and go against my natural inertia.

I'm now ready to join the flow of the hectic outside world.

OBSERVATIONS ON PSYCHOLOGICAL PHENOMENA UPON SPENDING THE WHOLE DAY IN MY APARTMENT—ALONE

Time

While I'm sipping my robust breakfast coffee for the day, still in my pajamas, I think of indoor activity—cleaning, writing, reading, re-potting plants, watching TV—something unsettling occurs. Maybe it's unity of space, lack of structure or distinct goals of active engagement which leads to the thought that there may only be passive engagement, ie. watching TV, one of my favorite pastimes—I even use a word which designates light use of time—"pass-time," which seems to be motion through time with no complex dynamic.

When thinking of this simple movement of the day, time as one dimension, not in interaction with others time seems to contract, get swallowed;

While it is still morning, say 10:00 or 11:00 a.m., I'm feeling that shortly it will be late afternoon, 5:00 p.m., or even evening, 8:00 p.m., and time for bed not long after that.

I feel trapped in a kind of time warp where rising in the morning and turning in for the night could become directly sequential acts, start of day and end of day as contiguous time zones.

This causes a vague, low-level angst, and impresses a feeling or even a deep knowledge of responsibility for the unfolding of one's own life.

An event while trying to create an aromatic ambience.

THE FLAME

I light my lavender candle for an inspiring fragrance. I look at the flames created by matches serving as the lost wick which are quickly using up their paraffin fuel, and burning brighter as they near the end.

The flames' motions are erratic—two flames merge and are playing—maybe obeying a law of thermodynamics or motion that I have no idea of. The two flames create a concave arc in the metal hollow for the tea candle, and are going back and forth at times going so high, making the melted lavender candle in the glass dish—above where I added real dried lavender and fresh basil leaf—simmer and sizzle.

I hold my breath thinking the glass might break, but I am helpless before it. I have to let it burn out, not blow it out.

In the midst of gazing with fascination into the flame I think of a clitoris moving to an unseen stimulation and the flame as the tongue itself. The flame moves like moist squirming flesh—both tongue and clitoris.

I think I might be breathing in toxic fumes from the high flames burning the metal which a tea candle's dainty frame doesn't do, but I sit fixed.

Then it goes out. The air becomes different, quiet as if a muse left.

WEDNESDAY — 9/11 COMMEMORATION A YEAR LATER

I wanted to be out with people, but as a single entity and anonymous. They were holding a service on the Brooklyn Heights Promenade, which is just down the street from my apartment. I decided to go at 12 noon when it started.

Grieving one year later captured the community imagination—do we blame the media or does it go much deeper? While I and others were respectfully milling about the promenade an overwhelming sadness came upon me. Its intensity took me by surprise.

It was warm and sunny, but the air was grey and silenced by the spirit of the dead with winds gusting over the landscape.

The eternal skyline on lower Manhattan stood stoically in the deceptive brightness—grand old family echoing the silence together, as one closing around the huge gaps left by their youngest, tallest fallen brothers.

The minister arrived—a pleasant youngish woman with long thick hair sensuously blowing in the wind. She looked Greek as her name on the badge suggested—Eleni-nice. She approached and asked me, "What brought you here?" I said, "I feel like I've had a death in the family"—which I have had many times many years ago.

Ripples formed in the stagnant pool of grief.

She said, "You have. Your family was stricken." She asked everyone to come and join hands in a circle. She spoke a few words and invited anyone to talk who wished to. I noticed some signs made by children hanging on the fence. One was a quote from Anne Frank, "In spite of everything I still believe people are good at heart." After reading this I spoke: "I hope and pray humanity will become wiser and have compassion and empathy come before everything." Words of everyday speech seldom suffice, but I think my tone had a note of desperation. People nodded.

I didn't feel hostile or angry—like I can and do—toward those who caused it. Sometimes it is possible to rise above, but only erratically. I felt the tragedy of being human.

Our ability to feel for others severs like a guillotined head when deep-seated fears and grievances come into play. The "otherness" of the offenders becomes foremost in our egocentric world, and common humanity becomes separated by an astronomical spiritual rift; violence can be inflicted with self-impunity.

Oh sure, the intellect—that shining hallmark of the human species—tries to talk the person into spouting ideals that we would like to exist as if they really do. I'm afraid the affective domain is the real one—and it's much closer to the animal impulse, the pack mentality. We can be predators so easily even if only in thought. Maybe it's a left-over instinct of kill or be killed. Only humans have added layers of symbolism on it to complicate matters—and always in the back of the mind somewhere nags mortality—the tragedy of being human.

I broke from the promenade group to go to an organ concert. When I said I had to leave Eleni said, "If you need to talk, my number is on the flyer. Give me a ring." I was touched and still depressed.

The stirring organ in the soothing low-light of the Episcopal church in high gothic style with its soaring grace gradually relieved my sadness. I guess music does "hath charms to soothe the savage breast."

THE GIRLS

The girls and I go way back. There's something important there. We grew up in the same working-class neighborhood in Queens—a boring little town of people with no imagination (as my aunt who only had a 5th grade education used to say). Many of them would live and die there in one long unbroken line—interrupted only by Fate's blows. Then there was our group. We would go to the local bar called "the Circus" that served green beer and bread on St. Patrick's Day. We were about 20 years old and shared an appreciation of insight about conventional behavior—not that we weren't conventional in many ways—we went to the local public schools, local churches and we wanted boyfriends and eventual marriage—but we saw through many artifices, especially with guys.

This was the early '60s when feminism wasn't formalized yet, hadn't coalesced into a social platform. Girls were supposed to listen a lot, not be overly knowledgeable or funny—we were supposed to defer to the guys for that, so we would pretend to be typical, follow the norm. When any of the local males engaged us in conversation I remember saying to Joe Blow let's say, things like, "Oh, I didn't know that" or "how interesting," and giggling as a woman in a satire—believable to the uninitiated, but with the girls it was an inside joke, and I reveled in their appreciation. I think we all felt peripheral to this small town society in New York and drew together.

It brings to mind a scene from the Circus Bar when a guy put his chin on his hands, and asked us if he looked sophisticated. Dolores and I and maybe one other girl were sitting with this guy at one of the tables in the dim atmosphere permeated by the aroma of brewery yeast. Beer was the drink of choice for the young people of the time and in that neighborhood. She went straight for the jugular and said, "No, more like a jackass." Not only was this out and out nasty, which sat uneasily with me, but also a betrayal of our standards of cleverness.

However, I didn't trust the girls. I felt they could also turn on me if there came a moment when the collective unconscious was galvanized from insecurity, self-doubt and a feeling of marginality. In an interlude at the bar of clever, ironic humor I felt I could come under the gun. I always felt vulnerable. Those were my easily hurt, victim days. Anyway I was the only one with a steady boyfriend, so I spent more time with him than them. And when I was with them I had a kind of tenuous, ungrounded sense edged with the thrill of an impending threat, a tinge of psychic danger, yet the communal understanding of a group of renegades. That's an exaggeration, but a good one. They were my choice rather than death by mediocrity—a strong fear harbored in my embryonic identity.

MOMENTUM

When she first met him at her cousin's house she was struck by the silence surrounding him. He had an intense fixated look as if stripping her emotionally bare.

His eyes always held the depth of his feelings in that bony, well-defined dark face which was a configuration of intelligence. She always liked the way his slow-eye had to catch up to focus.

After he moved in with her she would watch with fascination as his smooth tall well-formed brown body seemed to glide through the apartment even though his gait was really a giraffe-like loping.

He enjoyed walking naked. He was young and had a firm body. The male body had always been an inaccessible object of desire for her.

Intimacy with a male was a highly-prohibited wish—a longing never requited even during physical intimacy. It remained a longing unabated.

Her favorite moment was when they would bed-down for the night in the queen-sized bed—both naked. She would be against his back and felt the comfort and protection of that much larger body with a tinge of uneasiness around its ability to overpower.

She loved to form-fit her body against his back and buttocks; tuck her arms around his waist, body-cupping. She was half-giddy with sensuality and affection.

Love? Had it just been dissected? She loved to feel the soft brush of her pubic fur against his beautifully rounded ass.

He loved T.V. and sat on the floppy wheathusk-filled ottoman in front of it. She could never figure out why he liked Jerry Springer. "How can you watch that bunch of low-lives carry on like that?"
    He: "I think they're funny."
    She: "I can't look or listen to them for one minute."

She thought that watching them probably made him feel that his life situation wasn't all that bad. He had a job way beneath his capability. Life was difficult for him. He was afraid of it, deeply depressed. He often said, "I don't like life." She cried bitterly when he alluded to possibly ending it all.

It's intriguing how little human intelligence has to do with coping. She often thought he was brilliant. She didn't say that about many. He once said, "The creator likes to create, but then loses interest," and "Maybe there's really no god; we just don't understand enough about the chaos principle." They talked endlessly about creation, the world, human nature, animal life. This didn't help him live well.

One time she came home from work and found him still in bed, lying swaddled in the blanket, mummy-like. He preferred being at home, as in pupal stage. She liked to be out and about. Would he ever emerge from the cocoon?

She used to get angry and accuse him of not trying, not helping himself.

Sometimes, when he did agree to go out into the world, he would move quickly with determination to dress and get ready like building the needed momentum to be able to get out of the house as a rocket getting the proper thrust to leave the ground. It was almost comical.

She understands now. She never fully realized the gravity of his condition.

Now that he's far away and it's over, she holds the image in her mind's eye of his haunting grace and his slow eye catching up.

FAVORITE QUOTES

By people not publicly known

1. "Not only do you get old, you get ugly."
   —Lois Davis, mother of my friend Lenora

2. "No matter where you go, you encounter an infestation of humanity." —Jeanine Carr, cousin

3. "I'm a menace to myself." —Meryl Tubman, friend

4. "I often think of myself as a sociable misanthrope."
   —Carol Ann Nasta, yours truly

FAVORITE SONG LYRICS

"...Summer...Unashamed, she sheds her clothes."
"Tells the moon to wait, and the sun to linger;
twists the world round her Summer finger."
    —Theme from the film "The Summer of '42,"
      Michel Legrand

"The greatest thing you'll ever learn is just
to love and be loved in return."
    —"Nature Boy," Eden Ahbez

"Because the world is round it turns me on."
"Because the sky is blue it makes me cry."
    —"Because," John Lennon/Paul McCartney

"I'm in a New York frame of mind." —Billy Joel

"I don't remember growing older; when did they?"
    —"Sunrise, Sunset," Jerry Bock /Sheldon Harnick

www.ingramcontent.com/pod-product-compliance
Lightning Source LLC
Chambersburg PA
CBHW062227080426
42734CB00010B/2052